Privacy
and Intimacy

Mordechai Nisan

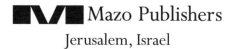 Mazo Publishers
Jerusalem, Israel

Privacy and Intimacy

*Cover graphic adapted from
My Dogwood by Nechama Leah*

Published by:
Mazo Publishers
P.O. Box 36084
Jerusalem 91360 Israel

Website: www.mazopublishers.com
Email: info@mazopublishers.com

Printed In Jerusalem, Israel

About the Author

D r. Mordechai Nisan, married to Malka and originally from Montreal, has lived in Israel since 1972. A captivating speaker, he has lectured before diverse audiences, including appearances on university campuses, television, and radio.

For many years, Dr. Nisan has taught Middle East Studies at the Hebrew University of Jerusalem in the Rothberg International School. He has also taught Jewish History and Zionism at the Orot Women's College in Elkana and the World Union of Jewish Students Institute in Arad, Israeli Politics at the Open University in Jerusalem, and lectured on the Politics of the Arab World in select Israel Army programs.

Dr. Mordechai Nisan

Dr. Nisan's extensive writings have dealt with Judaism and Israel, in addition to the varied peoples and complex politics of the Middle East. With a sensitivity to religion and culture, Mordechai Nisan offers a special prism of vision and reflection on the human condition.

Table of Contents

Part Two
Modern Themes

Introduction

I wanted to keep my privacy, though I sought intimacy with her. And when we established our intimate relationship, I didn't want to forfeit my privacy. Our intimacy, however, became for me a new domain of privacy, with our duality a unity. At the same time, my individual privacy did not dissipate, even when our joint intimacy blossomed and fortified.

We are born singly but are moved toward intimacy with another. We are born unaware of the existence of God, but then seek a connection with Him.

We are one and alone, free and unhindered, but consider that condition to be emotionally and socially intolerable. We reach out, knowing that it will deprive us of our full freedom.

We begin to comprehend that the complexity of human existence is an irony of compulsions wrapped in a dilemma of delusions.

I turn to the pages of the Bible and modern history to cull from them the materials for a commentary on privacy and intimacy.

We learn from the Bible that privacy can be a source of strength, and intimacy can be a pathway to fulfillment. But there is no magic prescription, for privacy can dilute the spirit, and intimacy can generate conflict.

Modernity offers agendas for privacy of the person, yet for emotional deviancy. The loss of authentic intimacy is often a mark of the era we are living through.

From the annals of public life we shall explore the ground of private existence. I hope that the end-result will enrich our personal consciousness and social contacts, without inducing friction between the two. A wholesome private inner world and a wholesome public outer world constitute complementary twin goals in the search for life and meaning.

An ancient Biblical verse conveys an ideal harmony of privacy and intimacy: "Love your fellow as yourself." This means that loving yourself is natural and legitimate and precedes loving the other, because you must first learn the art of self-love before you can cultivate love for another. The emotional chain runs from inside to outside, from privacy to intimacy.

Hillel, the Rabbinic Sage from ancient times, formulated a wise and succinct adage that travels the philosophical and moral route from privacy to intimacy: "If I am not for myself, who will be for me? And if I am for my own self, what am I?" Hillel teaches a person to first focus on personal welfare as one's individual responsibility, but then expects of the person thereafter active involvement on behalf of others. That involvement for others is, in its dialectic fashion, action that serves oneself as well. All this should be attended to now, conscious as we are in seeking a meaningful life and in search of good living.

From all this we learn that the search for meaningful lives and relationships of love requires both a certain wisdom and sensitivity. We must learn to accept the givens of our lives and build an island of serenity and a castle of happiness within them.

Part One
Biblical Themes

The Bible is replete with cosmology and theology, law and morality, history and mystery. It relates the plan of God and the whims of people in a constant repertoire of human striving that does not always achieve a level of performance at the level of requisite expectations and standards. The Bible is a book of life and real people.

The Bible reports the exceptional struggles at the heart of the human condition and subsequent frustrations and disappointments attending these authentic portrayals of mankind. In these stories we can learn about the essential contours of Biblical life which may also, in fact, contain the ingredients of our own personal lives.

In the beginning, before the creation of the world, God was alone in His privacy, before forming a relationship of intimacy with man. Yet intimacy with man did not signify the end of His privacy. Even when intimate with others, He remains bound and sealed away in His privacy.

It becomes the will of man to emulate this double "divinic" reality of privacy and intimacy, which is not a contradiction, but rather an expression of two poles of attraction, within and without.

1

Edenic Privacy and Paradisical Intimacy

Adam was the epitome of a man alone. No one preceded him, perhaps no one – he feared – would succeed him. Without anyone to the right or to the left, his voice and will could dominate the entire creation. He towered over the earth and his head could reach to the heavens. In the solitude of his existence, Adam was the sole master of all living beings around him.

Before man, there was God. No one preceded Him and no one would succeed Him. He commanded creation and was the Master of all forms of life. He was in the heavens and the earth, and His solitude set Him apart from all.

The solitude of Adam set him apart from animal creatures with whom he could not share any bonds. He was the governor of the earth that he shared with no one. His power was unlimited, his freedom unrestricted. On the planet earth he could enjoy the fullness of life, but alone.

Each one of us is an Adam in search of our boundless power and freedom. Each one of us seeks liberation in the private space of our own garden of unlimited access to the fruits of our choice and the delights of our fancy.

In solitude, Adam was called upon to probe the meaning of his privacy. His humanity evoked the possibilities of freedom, but also its existential confinement. Adam was made cognizant of his aloneness as loneliness. While the aloneness of God was a cosmic principle, aloneness for man was a symbol of the plight of the human condition. Man might have had everything at his feet and in his hands, but he was empty in his being.

And then God, considering that it is not good for a person to be alone, buoyed up the spirit of man as He extracted a rib from his body and presented him with the gift of a woman. Together man and woman, not just Adam and Eve, would contend alternatively with the inclination toward privacy and the touch of intimacy. Seeking one's inner self was to be forever entangled with drawing close to the other's self as two poles of push-and-pull implanted in our nature.

Without our privacy, we could never be drawn to intimacy; and without intimacy, we could never experience the loss of our privacy. We are one and two, and then perhaps a very different and special one whole, as our soul and body move toward and away from ourselves. We experience the adamic solitude as both pride and pain, and the genderic fusion as both completion and contraction.

Can we ever really know who we are when we are both one and two in the deepest recesses of our humanity?

2

Oneness of Man and Woman

The creation of woman from the body of man is a union, not just of the two sexes, but a unity within the natural human condition prescribed by Divine decision. Thus, the separation of man and woman is a function of the physical integrity of human bodies, a product of particularity, but not a denial of unity. The most profound natural state is one in which the connection between man and woman is primordial, awakening and imagining a return to that pristine condition of oneness.

Intimacy between man and woman – Adam and Eve – began at the moment that she was a physical part of him, just as such intimacy is consummated for man and woman, husband and wife, with the reality and return to this primeval fusion. This experience constitutes a virtual reliving of creation and its moment of unity, lending a dimension of trans-historical genesis to the act of physical bonding for all times.

Male and female are discrete halves of a divinely fabricated whole, destined by nature to search their transcending fulfillment in union. The very recognition of one's partial existence is an admission of a very private matter, moving toward discovering our comprehensive essence in intimate self-exposure and fusion. Man confronts his partiality in loving embrace of the woman who grants him the pleasure of unity.

3

Bonding
Mother and Child

The blessed fruit born from the intimacy of union is bonded from conception within the bearing mother. The unborn baby as fetus is never alone. Within the womb, the baby is part of the body of the mother-to-be. This natural union between mother and baby is evermore natural than that between man and woman - or Adam and Eve. An unborn child does not experience his own privacy because he is, at conception, intimately part of another being. There is no life without the womb of the mother nourishing and comforting the emerging fetus on its downward path toward birth - toward life.

The act of initial intimacy evolves according to nature's laws, concealed from any visible public exposure. Creation, as by God, is a hidden act. The creating act constituted by man and woman produces a result beyond human perception. Thus, deep in the womb, an unseen and exceptional relationship develops between mother and baby: one a part of the other, one at one with the other, and yet each distinguishable from the other. An intensive biological and emotional link will prepare for the appropriate moment when the fetus is ready to exit the womb and assume a physically separate life of its own.

And yet, the intimacy of mother with child retains a bodily connection through a natural feeding mechanism, that itself testifies to the incremental process of separation that does not isolate the baby from mother's nurturing role. In stages, the baby becomes a private entity, becoming a child and beyond, with the withering - but never elimination - of the bonds of intimate bonding with the mother. Only death, but often not even death, rents asunder the intimacy that began in the womb of creation.

4

Brotherhood and Rivalry

T he birth of Cain and Abel offers a promise of brotherly fidelity because the union of father and mother are the procreators of siblings from a common origin. The love and intimacy of the parents is followed, however, by the fire of jealousy and the first act of murder. Differences are intriguingly born from within the unity of one genetic pool. This mystery of rival brothers stains the genealogical cloth of unity and bonding born in a shared inherited descent.

Unlike man and woman, and mother and baby, the two sons never experienced integral physical union as one entity. Each was born as a separate child in physical and chronological uniqueness. The connection between the sons is provided by the family milieu, serving as a social setting in which privacy can intermix with intimacy.

The chance uniqueness of each child is not fathomed by scientific inquiry. It is a part of the spiritual and emotional underpinnings of the children when conceived by parents, their thoughts and character as unfathomable as the act of procreation itself.

Within the nuclear family, a constant search for solidarity struggles with a permanent aspiration for superiority. The intimacy of the family unit cannot easily be spared the intimacy of rivalry erupting among sibling members. Intimacy must be wholesome without smothering private space or crippling individual self-expression. The 'war of the brothers' among individuals and peoples is perhaps the saddest of conflicts and the most difficult to prevent.

5
Abraham, Friend of God

The exceptional spiritual giants whose every thought and action is concentrated on the Divine are necessarily men of solitude in society. They may be outwardly sociable and humanly involved, while yet concealing their inner private universe of love of God and submission to Him. Thus, the lone warrior for intimacy with God is a very private man. He is the friend of God, but he has no true friends of his own.

Abraham's human compass directs him upward and not sideways. He might seem outwardly affable and congenial with other people, and he no doubt was, but his spiritual eye was riveted elsewhere. Even when he left the Divine Indwelling to receive the three visitors who approached his tent, Abraham was not the kind of man to ever really depart from God. In agreeing to sacrifice his cherished son Isaac in fulfillment of the divine request, Abraham proved in the most exceptional manner his link to God above all else. Abraham could be as intimate as he was with God to the extent that he was private among men. Following the command to abandon his country and travel to Canaan, he had showed that God was his compass in life.

As he approaches the Divine reality, Abraham, the first believer and the friend of God, stands apart from mankind. While being the spiritual father of "many nations", he gives to all – even wicked Sodom – with never a need to receive anything from anyone. This was the thrust and purpose of his dealings with Pharaoh, and with Ephron the Hittite in purchasing a burial plot for his wife Sarah in Hebron. Abraham submits to God while doing good works for mankind.

The private cost of Abraham's monotheistic revolution is personal deprivation for a cause as noble as it is unconventional. He takes this hard road, along with Sarah his wife, and together and separately, they commit their lives to awakening in others the light of reason: meaning, the hand of God fashioned the world and keeps it in motion. Thus, intimacy with God can turn into a prescription of conflict with people, at times accommodation with people, inasmuch as the world is not always a ready receptacle for truth – reason and revelation.

6
Illicit Intimacy

The sorrowful isolation of Lot's two celibate daughters conjures up acts of illicit intimacy between them and their father. This sexual deviation is a moral perversion whose genetic impact cannot be measured or fully gauged over the generations. But the intention of the two daughters is nothing other than the worthy womanly-motherly mission of giving birth to a child. Nonetheless, one had the audacity to name her son *Moav*, "from father," exposing her father's paternity.

Lot, both father and grandfather, engages, unknowingly, in producing male seed through his own immediate female seed, in a reversal of normal generational and sexual behavior. Here the soft beauty of intimacy is mongolized in a passion of personal craving for self-actualization.

7

Brotherhood
and the Favored Son

Born of different mothers, Ishmael and Isaac are the sons of Abraham, but enemies of each other. The clash between them is personal and religious, with heavy moral overtones. Common fatherhood offers no foundation, as we learn, for brotherly harmony. Growing up in the intimacy of Abraham's tent does not either minimize or eliminate the incompatibility between Isaac and Ishmael. Rather it exacerbates the struggle of sons born from different mothers competing for the love and inheritance of their common father. Intimacy cannot be imposed from without, rather it must nurture and grow in a natural fashion among free compatible spirits seeking harmony and union as one.

The radical solution for conflict-resolution, and inadvertently conflict-maintenance, is therefore the expulsion of Ishmael and his mother Hagar. Abraham's bond with his son Ishmael is weakened, while that with Isaac is certified and confirmed. The promise of the land of Canaan becomes the private covenant for the seed of Isaac alone, born from Sarah.

The two sons of Abraham each receive the lot of their separate destinies, distinct one from the other, while bound by the legacy of a shared origin and the myth of a shared faith. History, ever since, is the record of this formidable beginning with yet no final end.

8

Clash of Twins

The twin brothers Esau and Jacob share the most intimate of primeval experiences within the womb of mother Rebecca. Their pre-natal condition, however, presages conflict despite the shared locus of natural origin. Biology is not adequate to blur the intricacies of psychology, as the twins diverge markedly in their character traits and personal fate. The physical limitations of the mother's womb, which may have forged intimacy, but yet compelled confrontation, set the scene for bitter and tragic sibling struggle.

Esau and Jacob represent the respective polar principles of physicality and spirituality, cast against the historical canvas of mankind's interminable clashes. The fact that the twins share the same parents, and moreover, the same womb at the same time of conception and birth, forges the powerful reality whereby such human beings maintain their individuality and need for personal space. Intimacy between two can breed a craving for privacy by each one of them.

Inner personal space naturally will seek expression in the external space that, if denied, can lead to an explosion of repressed wills and stymied ambitions. Sadly, Jacob and Esau are emotionally distant from each other when physically they are so close to one another. It was not by choice that they were placed in the same small womb of their suffering mother Rebecca.

9

Man and Women

The love of Jacob for Rachel follows the trajectory of the heart and not the pull of the body. It is the intimacy of soul lovers who know, by the spirit of their feelings, rather than by the closeness of their bodies. Within this intimate of relationships, the special wink of Heaven is the lovers' intuition.

With the unbending determination of one who cannot escape the chains of fate, Jacob exerts his body and invests his years for Rachel with but the seeming slightest of human effort. The intimate connection between the two is never diverted from the path of ultimate consummation, as the couple heads home. It is the quality and depth of their connection, not its quantity over time, that evokes the reverence of history.

Yet Leah, the second-rung first wife of Jacob, is loyal and central in producing the offspring of Israel. She hopes that marital intimacy will emerge, if not from instinctive love, then from instrumental performance. Leah gives birth to six of Jacob's male progeny. After death, a man's descendants remain to testify to his life on this earth. Leah serves Jacob well and the Jewish people are born.

While tension and competition mar the relationship between the two sisters, Jacob's spouses, reconciliation is not far away. They follow their husband back to his home and country, dutiful and loving. The seeds were planted outside of the land of Canaan, but the people's destiny always returns to its territorial roots in the chosen land.

10
Brotherhood and Reconciliation

The twelve sons of Jacob, who rear the twelve tribes of Israel, share the same father, though they are born from four different mothers. Competition and cruelty demolish the hope for brotherly fidelity. When Joseph is thrust into the pit and sold into slavery, the incipient and shameless hatred and jealousy of brother for brother knows hardly any bounds.

Yet the collapse of family solidarity does not end the possibility of renewal and reconciliation. It is in Egypt, not Canaan, that Jacob's sons rediscover the intimacy of togetherness. At that point we realize that while intimacy may be lost, it can be found and restored again. The contrite confession of guilt and seeking forgiveness can wash away the stain of an embroiled and vindictive past.

11

Mosaic Model of Aloneness

M oses, a most private person, is catapulted into the public role of liberator and lawgiver on behalf of the oppressed Israelite slaves. His intimacy is not with man nor with woman, but with the God of history and redemption.

It is the special and sublime character of Moses that is imprinted on the Hebrew slaves who are transformed into the free People of Israel. The Jewish nation is set apart from the nations of the world. Their special family genealogy and collective faith sustain Jewish national consciousness over the trials and tribulations of a long and harrowing history. At work is the religious chemistry of cultural intimacy among Jews with one another.

Under the leadership of Moses, the Children of Israel demonstrated unity at Mount Sinai with the giving of the Law and solidarity in the desert with the building of the Sanctuary. In these founding acts, the Hebrew nation was bound by powerful and intimate bonds of spirituality and generosity. Until today, the act of charity continues to unite the Jews, wherever they are found. The connection among Jews continues to represent a sacred trust, after more than three thousand years of a common history.

12

Universality and Nationality

J ewish peoplehood is both an event and a principle in the tapestry of humanity. Their history is paradigmatic, tilting back-and-forth between the amplification of universality and the exigencies of nationality. The twin poles support the edifice of national privacy and international intimacy over the millennia. The most private of peoples is likewise the most universalist of nations.

It was earlier that the three sons of Noah, dispersed across the continents, had become the progenitors of the varied and disparate peoples of the world. Separate peoplehood rather than one universal nation was the model of the international order. Thereby, the private lives of peoples were encased within the coherence and cohesion of distinct human collectivities. Loving one's own people would not imply, and certainly not compel, hating other peoples. But distinct lines of descent, particular languages, and special lands of residence, demarcated the map of humanity along specific boundary lines.

A person would experience the intimacy of peoplehood as a focus of identity and solidarity with his own kind. It was the Tower of Babel, with its presumption of one world and one language, that God considered a brazen rebellion against His single majestic rule. Peoples were many, but God was One.

Then, the One God fixed His covenant with the singular People of Israel. This chosen people was assigned the special responsibility to follow a clearly defined way of life among the multitude of peoples in the world. The Jews would internalize their Torah and pursue their mission with an inward impulse beyond the ken of external penetration. Theirs was a private venture in history and one in intimate contact with the God of Israel.

As a result, the ancient Noahide division of humanity was further highlighted with the explicit division between the people of Israel and the nations of the world.

13

Intimacy between People and Land

Portrayed as alone among the world of nations, the Hebrew nation is not to be landless on the planet earth. The Bible clarifies that the covenant between God and the people of Israel is rewarded with the granting of the land of Israel to the Jewish people. The sacred homeland is the prize for Torah observance. Intimacy with God is paralleled by intimacy with God's special land. To love God is to love God's land that was granted in contractual sanctity to the ancient Hebrew nation.

The conquest-cum-liberation of Canaan and its re-naming as the Land of Israel recalls the patriarchal promise of the land in fulfillment of God's will. But the military campaign of Joshua is also an act of national redemption beyond a vindication of the ancient covenant. Now the sons and daughters of Israel can finally live on their land as a free people. They are a territorial community acquiring a first-hand familiarity with the mountains and valleys of their homeland that will sustain their normal national life.

Joshua berates the people for their sluggishness in carrying out the conquest of the land, as Ezra later will bemoan the unwillingness of Jewish exiles returning to the land. It is part of the people-to-land connection that alludes to a less than diehard commitment to the geographic foundation of the historic drama of Jewish peoplehood. The tie to God seems almost to replace or marginalize the tie to the land.

It is the task of modern Zionism to retrieve from the archeology of Jewish memory the resonance of a love and longing for the Land of Israel upon which the State of Israel will arise from the ashes after a long lapse of two thousand years. Any readiness to normalize life in Exile, dissolving the people-to-land bond, is a violation of the special Jewish territorial intimacy with the chosen land. Abraham was promised the land and his children, moved by feeling and obligation, forever cherish their custody of the Holy Land.

14

True
Friendship

David, the shepherd from Bethlehem, remains alone and separated from his brothers to roam the hills of Judea tending the family flocks. But it is no less David the warrior who, with proud and intimate faith in God, confronts the giant Goliath and brings him down with a masterly use of the slingshot, not more. David is fearless before men because God is with him in battle.

It is the fortune of David to acquire the pure friendship of Jonathan, the son of King Saul, who unremittingly torments the harp-player and singer of God's praises. No degree of danger and personal risk can undermine the particular love and loyalty of two men – David and Jonathan – for each other. This is a mature commitment between manly souls in the name of justice. For the divine momentum propelling David to the kingship supersedes the right of Jonathan to succeed Saul his father as king of Israel. The special intimacy between David and Jonathan overcomes the biological father-son bond between Saul and Jonathan, who become enemies where jealousy and violence violate the paternal link. True intimacy between two people will always remain a secret mystery of souls and hearts, not of genes.

Even the lovers cannot comprehend the mystery.

15

Unity and Harmony in Jerusalem

King Solomon, son of King David, built the Temple in Jerusalem as a sacred locus of intimacy between man and God, and between the People of Israel and the God of Israel. The holy space of Jerusalem was the site for transcending the mundane level of human activities toward the spiritually uplifting climb to deeper faith and service of God. King Solomon declared that the nations of the world, not just the People of Israel, were permitted and welcome to come up to the mountain of the Lord.

This theme was later repeated by the prophets Isaiah and Micah as a messianic vision for joyous worship of God in the earthly habitat of the Holy Land. This majestic truth remains eternally true in Jerusalem. No other city in the world can make the extraordinary claim that "From Zion the Law goes forth and the Word of God from Jerusalem." The Holy City is one and alone in this divine regard.

The private affinity with the Divine could be the intimate experience and awareness of mankind as a whole. While serving God is a private affair and individual choice, it acquires an expansive quality when it is the celebration of religion as a communal, national, and universal act.

The Temple itself is a locus of prayer and sacrifice, feasting and law-giving. But it is foremostly the point on the world's compass for God's Indwelling to settle among normal mortal human beings on earth.

16

Flight to Privacy

The prophet with the most emphatic intent to maintain his privacy is Jonah, who fled from his mission, but in the end submitted to calling upon the inhabitants of Nineveh to repent their ways and do the will of God.

Jonah had chosen to refuse investing efforts on behalf of drawing this wayward Assyrian community back to God. He preferred to flee and conceal his identity rather than promote human repentance. Languishing alone on a ship, in a whale, or under a tree, reflected the solitary character of this prophet. His alienation from the gentiles of Nineveh was a consequence, perhaps, of a certain alienation from God his master.

17

Privacy as Solitude

J ob is a tragic example of a man whose private loss and malaise cannot be internalized by his closest of friends. While having been apprized of his sorrowful situation, they are unable to extend empathy to him. This is a human reality inasmuch as the physical separation between two people, and their lack of a common and shared situation or fate, can also carve out an emotional chasm between them. Only one in a similar tragic situation can more effectively extend empathetic feelings to a like sufferer. There is intimacy in suffering because the private pains are experienced as a common tragedy.

18

Hidden History of the World

The prognosis and prophecy of the ultimate end of days is central to the book of Daniel. But the details of the future are shrouded in difficult words and ambiguous calculations. We know that *the end* will come, yet we are not informed of it in a simple and explicit way. From this we must learn a very important truth.

The creation of the world, in the beginning, is one of the great secrets of the universe, and the end of days is one of the great secrets of history. At the categorical landmarks of time, God conceals the essentials of life. He is intimate with mankind only to a degree. He will divulge the path of human history, but perhaps not its terminus, and tell of its honorable characters, but not necessarily detailing all of their personal and private biography. He will set forth the basic law and the obligation of reasoned people to observe it. He will record the frailties of men and the nobility of individuals.

God will preserve privacy of knowledge and intimacy of intention. This is essential to a proper ordering of authority, without which, publicizing the private and revealing the intimate would wreak havoc in man and history. Like a measured vessel, man can absorb only so much in his human capacity for knowing and doing.

So too nature itself is ordered in a way that everything has its proper measure. A plant or tree requires a certain quantity and force of rain, and a sown field the appropriate sun rays upon the earth. So too a newborn child drinks mother's milk, but cannot yet digest solid foods. God in his compassion gives everyone and everything their portion of goodness for their benefit.

There are things, therefore, that we ought not to know, and this absence of knowledge does not signify a lack in our humanity. It is, in fact, the guarantor of our humanity, as a guarded and precious treasure. Proper living requires less than full knowledge in order to enable us to live our human lives.

The truly awesome dimensions of creation cannot be grasped by the human mind. The extent of the galaxies is beyond our comprehension. Most fundamentally, our mind cannot really conceive of the world prior to the creation of the universe just as we cannot conceive of how God came to be.

The program of history advancing toward the end of days is not fully known to us. Were we to be aware of all the stages and events along the path, we undoubtedly would be exasperated and terrified by some of the unavoidable processes unfolding before us. It is better that Daniel spoke in hints so that, while we know the end is coming, we are spared from knowing in advance the specific steps and their ramifications that will evolve.

A medical operation may be absolutely necessary and for the good of the patient. But the complications involved, the pain to be suffered, and the long path of recovery, could easily depress the most hardy of optimistic people. Better to know less and live better and, hopefully, longer. So too regarding the prophecy of the End of Days and our place in the script of redemption.

Knowledge can be a painful possession, and the limits that prevent us from acquiring more full knowledge are truly a blessing in disguise. The Bible conjures up man's place in the world while hiding the most private and intimate path human history will take.

The dramatic Biblical story of Bilaam, the prophet of the nations, conjures up the End of Days. He prophecies that in the immediacy of history "the Jewish people shall dwell alone" as a private collective experience separate from the peoples of the world. This is Israel's special destiny and Bilaam, giving voice to that which God has instructed him to say, blesses the Jewish people. And continuing with his prophetic parable toward the End of Days, Bilaam declares that "I can see it but it will not be now, I see it but it is not soon".

History's culmination is a principle of faith and a part of the Divine plan. Meanwhile, the Jewish people will conduct its life largely alone, in the privacy of its own path, in intimacy with the God of Israel.

Part Two
Modern Themes

Although man has reached the Moon, he is still perplexed on Earth. The anxieties and aspirations of Adam, experiences of authority and subjugation that he lived through, are the human condition until today. The enormous and sweeping changes that modernity has wrought in our lives do not alter, however, the predicament of life.

We now shall consider the question as to whether we most appropriately fit into the world of the Bible, or the world of modernity. Reflecting upon alternative principles and philosophies that modern history has put forth, we continue our search for the integrity of our privacy and the fulfillment of intimacy.

We necessarily and constantly seek our place in the world of identities and values. Our heart is our home, but is our home in the past or the present – or both?

It is always our good fortune that, possessing freedom of choice, we can choose and re-choose and de-choose. The ground of our existence is ultimately the freedom of our minds to decide our own independent choices concerning faith and behavior, identity and community, ethics and politics. We can look ahead or peer back into the past – or both?

Yet in truth, the distinction between past and future is an artificial distinction because the events and thoughts of the past permeate the present. The past is never lost and people maintain mentalities and memories rooted in the past, then drawn into the present-day of their lives. Our present is a time station between past and future. This is all we have, but it is everything.

For modern men and women in particular, the freedom to choose is a given procedural gift while the substance of our choices remains the crossroads we must pass each and every day in our lives. Nothing in the modern world is taken for granted, nothing is engraved with the stamp of sanctity and permanence. In modernity everything is a matter of modes and fashions that appear and dissipate all the time.

19

Master Man

It is common and conventional to believe that man and not God controls the center-place in the global arena in modern times. It is, moreover, man having displaced the Divine in history, who even arrogated to himself a primary place in the cosmic expanse of the universe. Landing on the moon and reaching toward Mars, man has squeezed from his superb God-given mind an insatiable curiosity and a genius capacity to explore the world that God created.

Man's creativity emerged from God's sixth-day creation in synthetic harmony, but human hubris. For the stupendous human capacities and achievements that modernity has displayed are at one and the same time a manifestation of God-given powers and a presumption of man-arrogated powers. Man's greatness proves God's existence and beneficence, yet challenges His primacy in life. Elevating man, however, need not demote the Divine in history.

Adam had been appointed the guardian and caretaker of the Garden, while modern man appointed himself the master of Paradise itself. He now believes, consistent with the idea that the Prime Mover removed Himself after the act of creation, that the course of events is in human hands alone. The cosmological theory of a God who fabricated a world for man was transformed into a humanistic theory that man, being the essence of creation, could dispense with the Creator. Thereby, the created being – the human creature – would ignore his origins and the dependency disclosed within them. Man would forget his genesis in order to travel the path of human greatness.

Here is a modern notion in a nutshell. Man looked ahead to the future and relinquished his own past.

20

Private Morality or Immorality

Adam hid in shame in the privacy of his sinful self-examination prior to being expelled from the Garden. Modern man would, however, affirm with pride, his private right to carve out his own norms of moral and social behavior, often in disregard of Divine commandments. Privacy is not just an escape route for modern man, but an ambiance for self-fulfillment.

While scientific questions are subjected to rigorous standards of truth and falsehood, ethical questions are judged by one's sensibility or inclination toward the good and the bad. Herein lies the great rebellion of man against any externally imposed code of behavior that is deemed by him inappropriate, unfashionable, perhaps oppressive, in any way or form. When man steps out from under the light of God's ethical doctrine, he necessarily takes moral lawlessness into his hands. While he cannot argue with the computation that two and two are four, he can contend, based on the autonomy of his moral judgment, that Adam had a right to eat whatever he chose in the Garden, that Cain's act of murder was justified by sibling rivalry, and that Jacob's sons were reasonably provoked by the self-aggrandizing behavior of brother Joseph. Once right and wrong as standards of evaluation are dismissed or ignored as the parameters of behavior, then everything and anything can be justified. In this amoral equation there is no philosophical foundation upon which to declare that Nazism was evil. It's all one's opinion.

21

Privacy
in Public

The pull of privacy is the aspiration of the body for self-identity. Man's obsession with his physical selfhood differentiates him from others. Medical research and advances, psychological analyses and theories, and aesthetic self-indulgences, promote each in their own way the intense expansion of the realm of privacy for individual people. Man's singular ontology – the nature of his being – makes him a unique self-consumed person riveted to his own welfare.

Western civilization espoused, under the motif of Greek physical culture, the exposure of the male body as a veritable work of art. This was illustrated in the gymnasium of Athens and in the sculptures of Rome. Exposing the body in life or art form was not an act of intimacy, but a radical assertion of pride of privacy in public. The shame of Adam was replaced by the shamelessness of man.

22

Privacy and Community in Faith

Both Abraham and Moses emerged as pioneer prophetic figures who knew solitude as the ground of religious encounters. God spoke to individuals before he spoke to the people as a whole. Nonetheless, neither asceticism and monasticism developed in Judaism, though it did become a form of spirituality and a strategy for survival for Christianity in a hostile and persecuting environment. Otherworldliness and powerlessness characterized early Oriental Christianity, while Torah Judaism knitted religion with family, tribe, nationhood, and mankind.

Religion lends itself to both private and public spiritual expressions. Yet, the public religious assembly is a powerful forum to unearth an emotional spirituality among the individual believers. One of the most surging manifestations of the religious experience arises within the brotherhood or sisterhood of prayer, song, and dance. This is fellowship in a sweeping collective form. The hearts of the faithful are bonded together, yet the private ecstasy and euphoria is the deeper experience. For we can never know if our personal magic moment of reaching toward transcendence is equally a magic moment for true human communion and a shared experience.

The private religious experience within early Christianity and some other Eastern religious movements embodied a significant message of personal faith and meaning in life. The public communal side of religion can definitely provide a context and be a catalyst for individual religiosity, but not ultimately an alternative to it.

23

Intimacy with God and Man

The search for the appropriate other, with whom to share a full experience of mind and heart, is in most cases a fruitless endeavor.

There is only a slim chance that two people can be in tune with each other on all matters of feeling, thought, and behavior. The hope for absolute intimacy and exceptional compatibility founders on the hard timber of humanity and its ineluctable and private individuality. All the sons of Adam differ necessarily one from another.

You may be at one with someone else in prayer and spirit, but not in social inclination and political philosophy. You may share a world of feelings for the human condition and its perilous tragedies and suffering, but be at odds with the other in intellectual matters and the topics of the contemporary agenda of life. Moreover, a man may be particularly compatible with a woman he loves, but with whom there are basic differences on broader parental child-rearing and family policy. It is unlikely that any binary relationship is fully spared moments of acrimony and anger, frustration and disappointment.

It is perhaps this distressing human reality that contributes to man's search for intimacy with God. Turning to Him assumes different dynamic spiritual and moral forms, from the trajectory to follow His ways, to the thrust to merge with His being. But the common religious ground draws from the recognition that the active pursuit of God in one's heart and in one's life is a formula for the Divine to enhance one's humanity. We seek God in order to affirm our humanity inasmuch as, without intimacy with Him, we are stultified in the quest for a satisfactory link with any other.

He, as the Other, offers a link that humans cannot reasonably or fully provide us.

24

Duality and Privacy

The division of mankind into different groupings is a product of the natural contours of heredity, circumstance or choice, and behavior. Anthropology identifies different tribes, sociology different classes, political science different power-seeking forces.

Judaism highlights the distinction between Jew and Gentile, and Islam that between Muslim and infidel. Manichaeanism differentiates the good and evil principles, Hinduism different castes, Hellenism the chasm between Greek and barbarian. Christianity identifies those saved by grace from those bereft of it.

It is not merely for analytic clarity that we identify dualities and the differences between them. Duality is a fixed attribute of creation, not just within society, or just between human beings. For at the beginning there was heaven and earth, night and day, land and sea, Adam and animals, man and woman. The embryonic structure of dualism in man includes body and soul, his life in this world and his reward or punishment in the next world.

The structure of our thinking, like that of society, follows the path of duality as individuality stands as an obstacle to the unity and intimacy of the opposites. Things are organized in pairs as a formula for both differentiation and unity, when things are more than a mere differentiation and always far less than a unity.

Inherent in this perplexing situation is the isolation or

abandonment of the person engaged in a permanent search for his complementary partner and mutual consummation. Virtually everyone and everything is only a part of a whole that may, however, never be found nor fulfilled.

25

Liberalism and the Loss of Community

The great burst of Liberalism beginning in seventeenth-century European history affirmed the quality of man, and perhaps the equality of men, in a bid to set them free for the individual pursuit of personal goals. Liberated from structures of power and authorities of faith, the individual could then choose his own private opinions and delineate his own life-style as an autonomous thinking and acting human being.

With the removal of public or collective rules and regulations, Liberalism granted people the right to their own thoughts and faith, expression and movement, in an unimpeded open environment. But this freedom elevated privacy above intimacy, individuality above community. This realization, painful and emotionally debilitating as it would tend to become, later encouraged a tendency to escape from freedom into the embrace of some repressive, if not totalitarian, political or ideological system. For a person is adrift without the anchor of wholesome relationships with other people.

The liberal mind was insufficiently sensitive to the need of people for emotional and intimate human contact. A personal liberation could become an imprisonment of the soul. Man cannot be free if bound by society, nor can he be whole or wholesome bereft of community.

26

Specious Species Consciousness

The rigor of classical Marxism demanded denying man his private needs and inclinations in favor of a leap of faith toward the unity of class and, later, humanity as a whole. For Marx, you must love all of mankind, but no individual person. In divesting oneself of personal passions and preferences, one is obligated to nurture recognition of one's belonging and submission to the human collectivity. One's partial existence is thereby transformed into species consciousness as personal identity submerges under that of the collective whole.

All of nature's bounty and all of man's artifacts and goods are the shared property of everyone. Each individual is summoned up to the sublime moral plane of feeling at one with the whole world. Everything that my eyes see and for which my heart yearns rightfully belongs to me. But everything that my eyes see and for which my heart yearns rightfully belongs equally to everybody else *too*. If it belongs to everybody, it really belongs to no one at all. Nothing is mine because my privacy, now suffocated by intimacy, has been reduced to nothingness.

When some hazard lurches in the public domain, I need not remove it for it is everybody's responsibility to remove it no less than mine. I therefore may wait for another person to demonstrate his species consciousness and social obligations, rather than bother myself with some problem that is of general public concern. Why should I pick up the litter in the park when it is the other person's park – and responsibility – too? Marxism, in promoting supra-human ethical standards, was the paradoxical agent for numbing the most basic human instinct of serving general public welfare.

Yet, it is the most natural and positive of human tendencies to seek fulfillment of our private welfare and personal satisfactions. We feel attached to what is ours alone, the works of our minds or hands, the connecting link between thought and product. Once we satisfy our private quest for creativity, satisfaction, and well-being, then we are buoyed up to offer public service on behalf of the community. Prior to that, our selfhood is constricted and our personal emotional well dry. But after that, we are rich in spirit, strong in confidence, and generous in will to contribute to others and their welfare.

Once enriched emotionally and materially in our private domain, we can turn to add to the enrichment of the public domain. Man is private not only or particularly as an expression of ego, but in the expansion of his soul on behalf of humanity. You cannot reasonably skip a stage in seeking species intimacy by bypassing the shaping and strengthening of one's own person. Only a strong individual can be a strong contributor to society as a whole. Individually strong marital partners can sustain a strong and healthy marriage.

27

Probing Privacy's Darkness

The development of psychoanalysis through Freudian research of man's consciousness and sub-consciousness is a voyage into the deep recesses of one's inner space. The private parts of man are not only his secret bodily organs, but include the hidden memories and thoughts of his personal past and unexplored present state of mind.

The attempt to chart the map of the mind pushes a person into the complicated and complex waters of one's formative biological and psychological history. Self-understanding to know oneself is not just an intellectual investigation, but a psychic search for self-awareness. Our personal origins are hidden from us, and our early infant period is concealed, and then forgotten. Even as adults we are unequipped to unravel all aspects of our psychic profile and its manifold behavioral ramifications. Self-knowledge is the key to our selfhood, though a mystery hidden by veils of impenetrable thickness.

The peering into the inner soul can be not only a vacuous effort with no revelation and no finality, but the entrance into a morbid narcissism of momentous psychic turmoil and confusion. A myriad of barriers separate us from ourselves. We bear within us biological-psychic or historic codes that may forever remain deep secrets. In the end, we are persons who are a mystery to others and no less to our very selves. This fact emerges when we discover within ourselves previously unknown great determination, talents, and productive energies in situations of adversity, or when we are exposed to our own outbursts of anger or violence that can appear as totally alien to our generally stable moral character.

The obsession with and within ourselves may turn out to be a venture of self-destruction more than a prescription for self-discovery and psychic tranquility. In a way, an excessively dogmatic concern with one's self is debilitating and stressful. We had better accept ourselves more or less as we find ourselves, try to improve our human qualities of patience, compassion, and generosity, and move on with the conduct of our lives. Inasmuch as life and mental health require solid relationships with others, the Freudian inner search can be a dangerous fall into an endless self-consuming pit of detachment from the social world that surrounds us. Better to reach out to others rather than delve incessantly into ourselves. We grab freedom when we remove ourselves from ourselves and allow distance to give perspective.

A person who confidently develops emotional balance humbly loves himself. This is never a step toward self-praise, or self-destruction, but fulfillment of selfhood alone.

28

Individualism Unbound

The school of Existentialism offers a radical route running from Liberalism to radical individualism. In the course of this trip, privacy is preferable to the entrapment of others. Self-affirmation and unbridled freedom were the starting-points, while egoism and misanthropy can become the last station on the road.

Such is the impulse of Existentialism toward an intense and complex self-examination into the depths of one's own inscrutable human existence. The person loses a sense of the inherent value and joy of life as such. His total preoccupation is inward looking, with a profound anxiety about his "being". What was once an awareness that Being was something outside of man now becomes an obsession that being is the essence of man himself.

The "other" as adversary is not the Divine above but the person over there. People are construed as obstacles to one's absolute liberty and any moral obligation toward them will detract from the unbridled choices or maneuvering of a free human being. Existentialism is therefore basically an anti-social doctrine inasmuch as self-knowledge relegates the other beyond the ken of the learning and living experience. Other people, not necessary for cultivating human intimacy, threaten my privacy and sometimes make my life not worth living at all.

This narcissistic philosophy cannot but isolate an individual from society and others. It is primarily a representation of an intellectual's haughty and puerile mental meandering into the depths of a concept. Detached from one's natural proclivity for human contact and community, the existentialist plunges into the nothingness of his constructs for the sake of clarifying his abstract being in a nihilistic world. From this will come confusion and depression, if not suicide, as the way of escape from the futility of life.

Existentialism, it seems, denies life rather than offering any insight or significance into its wonderful moments, special opportunities, and wondrous adventures. When all is said and done, our humanity is not designed for personal examination with an analytical research kit, but meant to evolve and unfold as life itself.

29

Women between Privacy and Publicity

The rise of Feminism demonstrated the collapse of traditional social norms and structures in favor of self-affirmative individualism. With radical abandon, women declared themselves to be single-minded people intent on achieving personal liberty. They acted as individuals who happened to be women, rather than as women who happened to be individuals, in forging their program for fundamental social change.

The women's revolutionary doctrine scoured the wellspring of identity for the privacy of their particular aspirations. This personal initiative was, however, detached from the private inner world of the woman, departing for the public outer world of the woman in society and politics. Modern women, frustrated if not embarrassed by their conventional role-playing, utilized their sex gender in portraying their basic identity with the hope to transcend it as a social disability. Here was an evolving formula for women's advancement in a way that the gentler sex would appropriate conventionally male public methods of struggle in the arena of political warfare.

The hidden mystery and attraction of women would be replaced by the public campaign and social drive for, at the very least, an equal status with men in society. But the historical balance sheet indicates that women failed to achieve full equality, though they did acquire far more opportunities. They perhaps compromised their special womanly qualities as partners of men in the building of sound foundations for the family and for general society. Alternatively, their social striving reflected female affirmation without tainting feminine allure.

Instead of being special in her own eyes and in the image of others, the radicalized woman now sought to be similar to men as joint producers of the social and economic goods of the world. This was not an enterprise to forge intimacy, but a private venture by one half of the human race in wreaking revenge on the dominant imperious male half of the human race. A pyrrhic victory would have been a more favorable outcome than the modern record of Feminism exercised on behalf of woman's progress, which could cast a shadow on happiness in marriage and the integrity of the family.

The advance of women's careerism focuses on female activity in the world, while ignoring the female source of the human world through her conceiving of generation after generation. A woman was in the past most private and partial in her roles, while the modern woman aspires to public and whole roles within society.

"Women's liberation" was a slogan with a cause that stood at odds with mountains of feelings and millennia of time. And while legitimate female grievances undeniably demanded male sensitivity and social mending, the female offensive was at the same time more a threat than a panacea to various social ills. Altering the order of society threatened the profound order of creation, according to which the beauty of being is stamped with perfect individuality and complementarity. Something sinister lurked within this revolutionary pretension of feminism: could a man maintain his traditional manhood in the face of the female assault on traditional womanhood? Tampering with conventional identities might unravel the cloth of social peace and sexual harmony in ways that, when we retrospect, the harm done may not be less than the advantages gained.

30
Body, Soul, and Intimacy

Pornography as a contemporary social fashion stands in stark opposition to the beauty and serenity of the private domain of the woman. Exposure of the body contrasts with the concealment of the inner soul. For man no less than woman, the emptiness of the spirit is itself resoundingly revealed when the physical is unabashedly flaunted for all to see.

The flagrant libertarianism characteristic of pornography serves to support in its paradoxical fashion the contention that women, in fact, are the true repositories of society's moral virtues. This was always intuited in traditional cultures whereby the female members stood as the symbols of sexual limitations and regulations. When she was pure, society was considered pure too. And despite this conviction, that the woman is the standard-bearer of morality, the man is not exempt from being committed to moral conduct in the domain of sexual relations.

But when a ruthlessly devouring culture taints women with lower standards and cheap appearances, the former norms of discipline and restraint collapse in the mad rush of sexism. Sex as an expression of love and as a mechanism for reproduction and continuity has been hijacked by sexism, as representative of elemental instincts divorced from human intimacy and purpose.

31

Privacy in the Modern World

Modern times have challenged the privacy of the person in manifold ways that touch our daily lives. Government has adopted numerous ways in our technologically sophisticated age to amass computer files of personal information about people. Television penetrates our minds and advertising programs our choices. Images evoke our imagination and the rhetoric of sophists manipulates our thoughts. Politicians seek to manage our preferences. Indeed, people are losing hold of the private space required for their own thinking and actions. The cellular phone invades our privacy wherever we are and the ultrasound test, while promoting prenatal health, peers deep into the womb before birth.

There is a gnawing sensation that people have lost control over their lives just when they have acquired extraordinary opportunities to extend the boundaries of their experiences and knowledge. We can see further, hear further, and travel further – more quickly and with minimum effort – than could have ever been foreseen in earlier eras. The machines of our age permit a fantastic diversity of activities and the money available facilitates the acquisition of a boundless quantity of goods.

Having more and doing more does not assure that we *are more* human in giving, loving, enjoying, or sharing the wonderful things of life more than our predecessors or ancestors on this planet. Nor does this mode of modernity promise that we can retain and cultivate our private inner space that is the home to our individuality and the rich potentialities ingrained in the resources of our DNA sources.

The rapidity of change and the speed of movement in modern society threaten the quiet and tranquility of our private souls. We need the pastures of solitude and the stillness of nature in this dazed-crazed world we live in. Bereft of intimacy with another or the Other, we have also seen the loss of our justifiably legitimate domain of personal privacy.

32

Culture Code Intimacy

Intimacy, by its elusive nature, is forged through a secretive code of communication between two people. This is not a matter of a signed contract or a guaranteed commitment. A relationship of intimacy is a complex web of symbolic gestures, expressions, and movements. It can be a whispering oral dialogue whose meaning is known only by the intimate partners themselves.

In the course of a marriage, the husband and wife develop their personal code of intimacy that binds them together in a unique fashion. They employ modes of communication that evolve from the integration of their separate personalities into a shared communion of feelings and reactions. A movement of the eye or a special glance, the use of a nickname or mention of a memory, can serve as signs that hint at intentions transmitted between the couple.

So too, does a nation, buttressed by an ancient culture code, solidify the bonds among its disparate members. For a culture is an intimate set of attitudes and behavior patterns that draw the unseen but easily read boundary lines woven around a given community of people. This code of culture cannot be learned by outsiders or fully penetrated by observers. The in-group is insulated by its code when its members enjoy the feeling of belonging to a select community that comforts them from the emotional ravages of life's travails.

The intimacy of a cultural code is not designed only to keep others out, though it does necessarily and effectively forge the links of sharing and solidarity within. This is the case for both animal groups and human groups, for large numbers of individuals and for smaller numbers of people. Indeed, the code that brings persons to respond instinctively to the melody of a song at a party, a chant at a sports event, or a ceremonial procedure at a religious ritual, is a force of social cement. In all cases we witness and warmly welcome the power of a sign whose meaning evokes the satisfying and acquired response we so relish. A national flag emotionally enwraps the patriotic citizens "around the flag", and one with each other.

People seek and need regularity and predictability in their lives. The culture code serves this human expectation by affording the symbolic mechanism to provide a shared world of meaning, without which we would feel adrift with unfamiliar people, in diverse situations and experiences, alone and bewildered.

Intimacy with nature is a feeling, but intimacy with people is a need. We cannot escape our fundamental humanity and we cannot fulfill it without the intimacy of other people.

33

Intimacy
in the Modern World

We are familiar with the social pattern in modern times of late marriages and early divorces, and few children per family. Yet the crisis of the family touches an array of questions concerning personal identity and collective purpose. Our morally disruptive age seems short on human commitment and solid responsibility. It reflects selfishness and narcissism, less giving and sharing, than in earlier periods of history. Personal expectations and demands are high, while generosity and forgiving are low.

The marital framework and institution is not properly utilized for building warm intimacy between a loving man and a loving woman. It certainly may be that people do not want to be alone, but neither are they particularly capable of becoming truly intimate with another person – even with the one they marry.

The basic problem is that the swirling pressures of modern life, along with the fanciful attractions that plaster the billboards, media, and films we see, overwhelm our sense for moderate judgment. We find it hard to be satisfied with what we have – like our marital mate – when confronted and mesmerized visually with appealing alternatives. But the alternatives are not personal options and, almost always, a temptation that cannot be fulfilled.

So we must decisively concentrate our perception and energies in order to enjoy our privacy and shape our intimacy with the other into a healthy and satisfying relationship. Do we know what it means to be intimate with our marital partner when we are diverted by dream-like fantasies from near and far?

In modern times, we are being transported out of our native selfhood and removed from the reality of the personal parameters of our life. Looking into the mirror is the start of knowing oneself, and peering into the soul is the foundation of self-recognition.

34

Privacy and Silence

The intimacy of life is best mediated by silence. Discourse between human beings can take place by unspoken and shared thoughts flowing among mind-bound individuals. Prayer from man to God ascends from earth to heaven in meditation and whisper. Non-verbal communication between humans is deep, without words serving as our receptacles of musings and ruminations.

The life of a recluse or the ways of a lone wanderer reflect the ultimate rung of private existence distanced from human society. But, more than a statement of personal purpose, it demonstrates an extreme divorce from fellowship and community. A one-sided lifestyle is an imbalance of the soul without society.

The corruption of modern language is a rampant destruction of proper grammar, adequate vocabulary, and civil speech. Part of this linguistic deterioration derives from the massive assault of visual media communication on human beings. Raucous music also contributes to the dulling of our mental faculties. With less inclination to think, and a poor capacity for intelligent talk, modern people living under Western influences have lost something essential about what it means to be a human being living in human society.

Unprepared or unable to cultivate a healthy ambiance of privacy, we may fear slipping into loneliness and isolation. Largely unequipped intellectually and emotionally for being by ourselves, we cling aimlessly to the blinding images and deafening sounds of a consumer culture that threatens to cheapen our spirit and paralyze our mind.

Silence is not therefore just a non-verbal form of behavior. It is also a special form of private human tranquillity and intimate social communication. We live in a world of awesome noise: it reverberates incessantly into every corner of our lives. People may think that silence belongs only to sleep but in modern times, with electronic modes of noise making, we would do ourselves justice by introducing a bit of silence in our waking hours as well. If we would speak less and do more, the world would be a more wholesome and better-ordered place to live in.

35

Privacy and Leadership

In privacy, calm. In intimacy, comfort. The inner world is the foundation and gateway for the external world. A great leader grows and emerges in history after he has passed through a period of moral and spiritual incubation. It is in such a person, like a plant buried under mother earth, that we witness the beauty and strength of a full-grown human being to stand and lead a people.

A great leader never seeks nor solicits leadership, but rises to such a position of responsibility as a natural process. His education and training become a stepping-stone for public service. All rich and thoughtful cultures have recognized that leadership begins within the stages of an individual's private life. Beyond the eye of society, a single person acquires not just knowledge and experience but, most importantly, a self-consciousness of himself and an awareness of the world around him. The true leader is in touch with himself and bound to the people.

It is therefore the private inner domain that girds a person with calm; and it is then his public external domain that binds him to others. He is the giver of comfort to the forlorn and the weak, the helpless and the hopeless, of society. The leader's inner world is buoyed by access to the heights of possibilities that his imagination can reach. He knows that the givens of life are only one of many alternatives that all people, properly guided by the leader, can reach. The leader, as teacher, can shape the lives of followers and, thereby, alter the world we all live in. He does it for himself and he can do it for others.

36

Human
Intimacy

People living in modern times, sometimes lacking an indigenous community of fellow denizens and cherished friends, sense the abandonment or *anomie* of mass society. Thrust into life's incessant turmoil, we cannot feasibly acquire all we want, when we want, at the price we want.

More foreboding is the inescapable given human condition: that we ultimately do not control all aspects of our lives and their precarious and unforeseen developments. We are flung into situations, we are the victims of circumstances. We cannot heal all our ills, we cannot guarantee the fulfillment of all our hopes. Life is stronger than any program or plan we have devised for it.

Because of this reality of unbearable pressures and unrealizable expectations, people seek the soothing compensation of a relationship of intimacy. In modern society, folk cultures and ethnic solidarity may crumble, religious fellowship and vocational camaraderie may decay. Wherein lies the fountain of life to fill the empty vessel of our soul?

When an individual participates in the intense interaction of a small group, he can acquire the strength from the outside to resuscitate the lethargy within. We ought not to dismiss the moral and social efficacy of an intimate literary circle, bowling league, army unit, prayer community, card club, or exercise course, to provide us with the energy to push on with the challenges and disappointments of life.

A human being needs not only *meaning in his life* but also *people in his life*. The magic of intimacy is a healer, not only for lonely souls, but for all individual souls.

We cannot estimate or easily measure the scope of our human capability to feel for other people and be tied to them, be they of our own nationality or religion, social station or territorial enclave, or not. People are spiritually programmed to be able to establish an instinctive and immediate bond with total strangers whom they never knew until a minute ago. A chance meeting or an inadvertent conversation can break down barriers between people. It is the connection of the eye or a generous smile between two people that open up the spiritual pores for comfortable human communication.

The intimacy of people is evoked at work, at a sports event, amusement park, ocean beach, public lecture, movie theater, or vacation site, as a matter of course. We do not in particular reflect on this phenomenon and seem to think it is of no special importance. But this extraordinary and unplanned intimacy among people testifies to the innate goodness of mankind. People can be intimate with one another, no less in a fully extemporaneous fashion, because they are generally good in heart and generous in spirit.

We are drawn toward other people as friends and lovers, neighbors and colleagues, in countless ways in the course of our lives. And we should be conscious of the wonderful fact that we discover our profound humanity in the magnetic nexus of relations of intimacy, of whatever significance and longevity. It is absolutely clear that just a momentary conversation with a passing pedestrian, or between two tourists in a holiday resort, proves that people need people and can feel comfortable with people without any prior preparation or anticipation. We belong to the common fund of humanity.

We may somehow sense that the intricate programming mechanism enabling and drawing us toward human intimacy has been installed in our spirits and souls, hearts and minds, since the beginning of our species history.

Closing

We end our inquiry of privacy and intimacy with the 36th chapter. Evil and ignorance fill the corridors and corners of the globe. Therefore, the ultimate fate of the world rests upon the enduring goodness of certain special people who are often not known, remain private and humble, and whose virtuous actions are unrecorded. Their mission is not a secret stratagem for victory, but rather a sacred responsibility for salvation. It is their lives that bestow upon us all the blessings of life. Their privacy is born of an intimate concern for others, just as God showers upon people untold daily blessings without any formal declaration or visible sign of Him doing so.

In Judaism, the number 36 appears when identifying these righteous individuals *(tzadikim)* and men of judgment who seek "divine" kinds of knowledge. The arena of struggle for them is not human confrontation, but one of intellectual striving for special enlightenment.

The number 36 also appears as the majority required to pass judgment in the ancient High Court sitting on the Temple Mount in Jerusalem. A Biblical source for this comes from the time of Moses in the Sinai desert, when organizing the 70-member judicial governing body of the Hebrew nation. Each member was to be of the highest moral, spiritual, and intellectual quality. A 36-member majority rendered judgment based on wisdom and public legitimacy. Righteousness and law were to flow from the legacy of Sinai into the sanctuary of Jerusalem.

Law must be endowed with righteousness, everywhere and for all times. But if the Court of Jerusalem is temporarily inactive, and the Law is momentarily not shooting forth from the Holy City, then at the very least humanity is blessed with 36 righteous people. The universal court of salvation is operating for mankind through the righteous 36.

Seeking God is linked to serving mankind. The meritorious deeds of the 36 righteous people provide the moral foundations for humanity's survival. The survival of the world as a whole, not just one country or people, is the highest goal. The full measure of good deeds is not ever fully known. This too, apparently, is part of a concealed calculation registered in the heavenly account.

The unseen represents the domain of true purpose and the reality for ultimate action. One way seeks intimacy for one's own inner coterie of people; the other way projects intimacy for the welfare of all. There are intimate modes of love, assistance, and friendship that are not publicly known, but are no less effective and sustaining for other persons' benefit.

The person who purifies and perfects his own righteous qualities and actions becomes a messenger of righteousness to the world. Certainly, that person spreads the light, warmth, and glow of righteousness to the people around him. Living for oneself and for others becomes the path to a fulfilling and harmonious life. Anyone of us can become one of the 36 righteous people serving and saving the world each day.

To affirm and enjoy one's privacy does not nullify the option of being open to people and in loyal solidarity with them. Privacy and intimacy are different modes of living in a comprehensive human reality.